SCRAWLED STARS

.

Scrawled Stars

Lianne M. Bernardo

First Printing: July 2019

ISBN: 978-1-7750431-3-3

Note about the font: The font featured in the titles on both the book cover and at the start of each poem is based on my own penmanship (when writing in print).

Write, write, write:
write until all the feelings come out,
words made manifest

NOWHERE TO HEAL

How do you heal
broken souls and
shattered hearts?
There's no emergency room
for those kinds of diagnoses.

THE REST OF US

We often speak of the strong—
those who are unafraid to bleed—
but what about the rest of us?
Too shy to stand up,
speak out, and push back;
where does that leave us?

RAGE

There is rage,
a clawing sensation
ripping through invisible echelons.
It will not be reigned,
it will not be silenced,
it will shred every
decent object in its path.

All Dues

Good things do not happen all at once;
they buckle and crumble by the weight.
To those who are patient all dues are rewarded
whilst the rest of us churn and lament
and learn to wait under duress.

THE ASSASSIN

Old age is not some dowdy fellow,
the kindly dame with a smile and an apple.
No, old age is a beast with claws
ready to pounce and ravage the remains of life,
tearing at the remnants of clarity, vitality.
Old age is an assassin walking in twilight,
its killing hand slow, debilitating.

A CAUTIONARY FALL

A lunge face-forward,
headlong into the abyss
cannot mask the
furtiveness, the concern
associated with the
fall.

SKYWARD ORBITS

Ephemeral clouds
illuminated by an unbeknownst rainbow.

Shy stars mask that
which they make them glow.

And all the while waiting
for the unsuspecting fellow
with the key to unlock
that orbital meadow.

END OF IGNORANCE

Conspiring with monsters
     poorly veiled,
we throw our futures away
     with a single stroke.
Wave goodbye to blissful ignorance,
     comfortable stagnation—
what is witnessed cannot be erased
     from sight,
     from mind.

UNKNOWN TERRITORY

Like timid stars failing
to light the dark expanse,
my courage falters.
The outcome is veiled to me—
no moonlight to lay bare
this untrodden path.

LIFELINE

Is there a lifeline for timid hearts?
A reprieve from offsets and restarts,
shelter against a thunderstorm.

YONDER

What spherical delights lay yonder
the grey soot of clouds?
Spring is but a stone's throw away
past the frosted chill,
the invisible slab of ice.

SORROW'S COURSE

Long sorrow flows
from an everlasting rainspout:
it spews come the heavy rain,
it trickles when the sun is out.
It never ends, it remains open,
always leaking, always pouring,
never ending...
Life is never the same.

AN ABSTRACTION

There is silence where there should be stars
blossoming against the night-time canopy
but they have failed to shine, shy little light bulbs
put out by creation's ongoing tragedy.
How best to coax them out of heavy dreariness,
promote the joys of life, not pathetic fallacy?
But there is no celestial rainfall for this sort of growth
and   all   one   is   left   with   is   abstract   strategy.

STORM

The old church steeple
shudders against the howl of the wind,
the clamour of the rain,
whilst the faithful beneath
its arched wooden beams
look on in anticipation.

YEARNING

It is a sombre day,
a day for mourning clothes
and funeral dirages.
I step through the threshold
half-expecting her wandering
   self to greet me
only to find emptiness,
and absence,
and a shocking lack of pink.

WINTER (Part 1)

Winter is for the solitary,
to those who need silence in the world;
they walk along fresh banks of snow
their footprints deep, alone.

WINTER (Part II)

Winter is for the patient;
they wait indoors for the frost to end,
for when the snow melts
spring will come forth.

TIME

There is no time to make
but time to take;
no choice between one or the other,
it gives only what it can break.

THE LENGTH OF LOVE

For the length of love
goes on and on forever
even after forever ends;
it may fall asleep,
it may lie low in
dejection and disarray,
but it will never end.

A CENSURE

Stranger, lend me your tragedy
to mask my own disappointments,
balm my cumbersome hurts.
For moving forward is like
wading against a hurricane:
the water pushes me to my knees,
fills my lungs with sea salt,
and I bear no life raft.

PALLBEARERS

Sadness is the name of my
   handmaiden, my pallbearer;
   her tears are my tears,
   her sorrows a reflection of my own.
Her cousin, Regret, stands on guard
   to deliver the eulogy
   of all my unfulfilled dreams
   and of my heart's desire, denied.
Disappointment shall be the
   funeral forecast
   to mask the rays of hope,
   push back possibility to another day,
   give the heart time to grieve.

BLINDNESS

The faithless flock
to where there is no relief
only endless dissatisfaction
void of all belief.
What cure is there
for the willful blind?
They wander and they search
but they will not find
what they seek, only achieve further grief.

TRANSITORY

Time is ticking,
we all have somewhere to be;
all an illusion
everything is transitory.

AN INVOCATION

Hear me, O blazing sun
that scalds the earth
and warms my muse:
my love and I have been
torn asunder,
bereft of all joy and
only sadness is left to plunder.
Merely shadow and memory remains,
poor imitations of before;
there is no return
old paths broken beyond restore.
Little hope crackles on
—for after the long night comes dawn—
but time is a·ticking,
precious feelings may soon be gone.

MUSE IN ABSENTIA

Where has my muse gone?
It went away, disappeared beyond the dawn,
leaving me with such great stealth,
and words not wholly heartfelt.

WITHOUT A TRACE

And when I get up and leave this place
I fear it'll be as though
I was never there at all.

STRANDED

There are no certainties in the dark;
helpless as the stranded I stand
blinded without a North Star
to illuminate a path forward.

RETREAT

Enticed by a golden prize
I'm awarded instead by
   an empty box with
   all promises vanished
   replaced by anxiety
   and unwanted heartbreak.
All my champions have fled;
alone I bear no compass,
   no shield against the wolves
   and invisible monsters
   that lie in my wake.
I crawl back to safe havens
   in solitude.

BROKEN STARS

Stars can break too:
they are just too far
for us to notice.

COMING OF SPRING

I wait for spring
to thaw winter's dredges,
uncover hidden derelicts
waiting to be cleared
paving way to
blooming flowers,
organic hope that there are
beginnings after sad endings.

POWERFUL

Beneath aloofness
and a picture of detachment
lies a soul that has weathered
every anxiety thrown her way
by the world.

I am powerful.

EXPLORER

Are you flying or are you swimming?
   they ask.
I am both, I reply,
   flying through unknown airspace
   beguiled by westerly winds and stormy weather,
   swimming through uncharted waters
   floundering amidst an array of sea monsters.
Air or water, it makes no difference;
   the motions are the same, the cold and frost are one.

BEFORE THEIR TIME

Timid little stars that fail to shine
for more than a few seconds at any given moment;
they were hastily stapled against
the celestial heavens before their time,
fated to huff and puff until their light gives out.
Eternity does not factor into their thoughts;
the spaces between them remain an empty void.

SOL IN ABSENTIA

After several days of
dark skies and cold frost
the bright star shows its face,
bombarded with questions
as to its whereabouts.

It was too lazy, it seems,
to rise up those days,
thus leaving the absconded
earth waiting in the dark.

NATURE'S ANSWER

There is resilience in nature,
against the forgetfulness of man.
It rebels with age-old rage
   —coal-fuelled clouds,
   and claps of electricity,
   rushing waters and
   deep earthly shudders—
to which we mere humans
can only stumble through
until the anger clears.

END OF DAY

The limbs of the tree are decorated in pink,
swaying gently in the warm spring breeze,
a picture of contentment against the
last rays of the day's sun.

SUNBEAMS

How does one
gather sunbeams into one's arms?
They burst and scatter,
strong and delicate,
any and everywhere,
leaving empty hands
and warm memories.

SOUL

The river of my soul came apart,
branching off to little streams that trickle
to which I no longer recognise—
the world is undone.

FOREVER

What do I know of forever?
Forever hasn't made itself known to me.

ANCHOR

The eyes look afar:
—a story calls
—a mountain beckons
—a road pulls at my feet—
but the thing is:
I always come back.

NATURE'S TRICK

The gentle sun
lends its own little trick
to those not well-versed:
clear blue skies do not reveal
the cold snap that settles yonder.

HOSTILE ENVIRONMENTS

The world is already
  a frightful place
  a confused space
  a troubled base—
Why do we make things
  more difficult?
Why do we place fear
  before trust,
  hurt before help?
Why do we eat our young,
they who are still making their way?
There are no answers:
only rage and thunder and
  a call to action.

HEALING

The sadness
buried in your chest
will dislodge itself
one day.
You will feel joy again
someday.

INSOMNIA

Sleep evades
like a thief in the night.
The moon is hidden
and the roads are quiet.
Yet the mind goes on
and on and on...

WORDS

Writers speak of words
like water, like petals,
like rain
that ebb and flow
and dissipate away.
But words are like stones too
that we hurl to one another,
lay down and build our houses,
set before us like anchors.
Words are strong like that.

UNSUSTAINABLE

This hope cannot be
anymore sustainable
than a vision in the desert,
a snowflake in the dead of summer,
a flicker of light in the dark.

NOCTURNAL SALUTATIONS

Hello, night:
your silence beckons,
your darkness calls,
a safe haven of some kind,
a canopy of possibility.

GRIEF (CON'T)

Loss
and its anchored pain
never lessens,
never dulls—
a well of tears
rises up like the tides,
the moon a glowing orb
encapsulating the
hollowness,
blazing in its reminder.

GUILT'S ERASURE

Mercy in the hereafter
is not enough to
erase the guilt;
hindsight is a prison guard
that shows no reprieve.

ROMANTIC VISIONS

There is still romance in the world
such as when the violin trills
and paints a portrait
of a moody landscape
with desolate, silent trees,
ombre clouds cast over the land,
a lone bird slicing through the air.

ADULTHOOD

Time and love and death
pulls old friendships apart,
an echo where they used to stand,
unbreakable pillars they once seemed.
Perhaps this is what
adulthood is all about.

A REMLNDER

Friend, can't you see
the precarious space you're in?
It's not always blue skies,
green fields, red roses;
there are storm clouds
and lava fields
and bushels of ivy
along the road too.

DAWN

Daybreak lies on the horizon
but the light is slowly dying,
gone before its time,
dead on arrival.
Until then the faint sliver
of hope glimmers,
just as the rest of the lights
flicker out.

HALOGEN

The halogen moon
and the makeshift stars
hang aloft a deep, dark well,
the stuff of mystery
and concern.

BENEATH THE DEPTHS

Peerless blue skies
do not always reveal
the depths of troubled waters;
the blue conceals the blue
like a porcelain mask,
a great smokescreen
of mist and thunder.

THE SECOND ELEGY TO A.R--

Your absence is
an oasis of sorrow.
Your lack of here is
the desolation of now.
No amount of funeral songs
can express the deepest of sorrows;
no amount of prayers said
can bring back the triumph of yesterday.
But there is no toil in the hereafter,
no pain can touch you now.
Rest easy, dear cousin, rest well—
love is forevermore,
let our prayers be unto you
a sweet lullaby.

ELECTRIC ORBIT

The electric sun and
the halogen moon make
their merry little dance
along the wire above,
the dark-rimmed eyes
and the absent smiles below.

CONSOLATION

Little heart, be strong:
the wide world is populated
with hearts made of
sand and concrete,
neither steadfast nor soft,
with true flesh and blood
but diamonds hidden
in well-folded corners of stone.

METAL DREAMS

I am young copper
still fresh to the beatings
and moulding of external will.
I am new metal dreaming
to be strong steel,
to stand the test of the elements,
bowing to no foreign request.

UNWANTED VISITOR

It is a prickly sort of fellow,
this hollowness I feel:
it shifts and morphs
and is difficult to placate,
difficult to heel.
It does what it wants,
it comes and goes when it pleases,
a visitor unwanted,
a wanderer who won't leave.

ON LONELLNESS

No, I never felt lonely
wandering amongst the
overturned rocks and
the silent mountains.
They greeted me like an
old friend long absent,
the vast tundra welcoming
my heart, my silence as theirs.

SUMMER (Part 1)

Summer
is for the blooming of love
expanding like the long sunny days
outstretched along the horizon.
Their warmth lingers
as memory long after
the time has passed.

SUMMER (Part ⅠⅠ)

Summer
is for the melancholics
remembering sunny days passed,
of happier times when love
was still new and still present,
gone before the first chill
has settled.

GRIEF (CON'T)

Fresh grief
falls like new snow
on a clean landscape:
it numbs before
it sinks in.

SORROWFUL WEATHER

Bright starts
pave way to
mourning shrouds
and funeral songs.
There is not enough
rain in the sky
to cover the wake,
express this sorrow.

WHAT MATTERS

It is in moments of sorrow
that you remember
—to say the words that matter
—to do the things that matter
—that every moment matters.

EARLY FROST

Evergreens turned to frost too early,
and they've only recently bloomed
once more.
Winter has settled early this year,
the sun's rays won't touch no more
(all the warmth of cotton spun
won't shield oneself
from the cold).

NO REPOSE

The lilacs ropes are burning
and the chains in your mouth
are dripping with blood.
What repose is there
when the storm is swinging
down the valley
and there is no place
to hide?

MISTS

The mist descends
blanketing the land
like an opaque shroud
but it cannot conceal
the glow of the mountains
cutting across the mood
of the land like the sun.

DODGEBALL

I saw the sun
trespassing
in a cloud-filled horizon.
I saw the moon
hiding somewhere
along the night plateau.

FINAL BREATH

Forever lay on the lips
of those not quite so dead,
their hearts still stumbling
long after their lungs gave out.

LOSING YOU

Friend, I'm losing you
to mounds of dead trees
and cramped hallways
and people with question
marks, faceless to my
recollection.
Sisterly bonds have
weathered storms and
floods and dirages,
now reduced to a few
words, decided nothings.
Friend, where are you now?
Empty space lies
where you once stood.

FRIENDSHIP ENDS

And maybe in the end
I'm just as much bound
by solitude as the next,
that all bonds of friendship
come and go like
the settling of rain
on arid lands.
They wax and they wane
and you are left staring
at an ever-changing sky.

STEPFORD

I don't recognise you any more:
your words stand so brief,
your laugh echoes hollow,
your presence an absence on the walls.
How did it come to this?
Who is this person that stands before me?

FRIENDSHIP ENDS (CON'T)

Relationships can die
with a bang or a whimper,
with a seismic earthquake,
or the most of ordinary of
the everyday.
It makes no difference though:
death is still death.

BRAVERY

If only I were brave enough
to say out loud
all the things I whisper
in the dark,
in the silence between moments.

SYNTHETIC ENVIRONMENT

Make way for the polyester sky,
the two-toned sea that's labelled
hang to dry;
can't have machines shrinking
those latex clouds into
tiny oblivions, useless and
ready for discharge.
Time to pin the sky up for the day,
illuminated with electric lights,
LEDs, long-lasting until it
hits its delivery date.
Until then, permit me to rest
until it's time to furl up the sky,
and make way for the LED lantern,
hanging low amongst pinprick stars.

FROSTED MOON

A half-frosted halo
surrounds the moon
bearing an ominous message
of the cold to come.

FIERY

The stars are on fire
but there's no one
to fan the flames.

FRIENDSHIP ENDS (CON'T)

This is what losing feels like:
the silence where laughter once echoed,
the void where thoughts once flowed,
the sudden loss of a comrade in arms, a friend,
and the freefall the comes right after.

UNA BELLA GIORNO

The last beams of the sun,
stretching across hot clear skies,
sets on the eternal city,
engulfing marble walls and
terracotta roofs in gold.
Behold as evening sets on
the chaos of the day,
the derelicts of a remembered past,
the coming night with
all of its mystery.

A DREAM

I dreamt along whispering shores
under a canopy of dreaming stars.
The waters whisper its nocturnal lullaby
against the stillness, the silence,
alone save for the observant night sky.

LUCK & EFFORT

They say I am
the architect of my own fortunes,
but the luck that runs with it
is not born of me;
the extent of my failures
is not wholly my own.

SUMMER (Part lll)

Summer is for the joyous,
the warm radiant days
reflecting the light in their hearts;
the day stretching well into dusk,
delightful days everlasting.

NIGHTTIME BANQUET

The harvest moon makes it
grand entrance,
lazily hidden by a wisp of cotton,
bright light reduced to a hazy glow.
Where are the stars tonight?
They seemed to have turned down
their invitations,
opting for a night in over a
slow swan song.

FILLING THE SPACES

Let us share trivialities
with what little time we have;
bemoan our surprising scars
with but small space between us.
Our muscles stand still, bones
erect as monuments,
easy silence and hushed presence
      —this is all we have to keep.

NO LONGER NEEDED

I've learnt in the saddest
and most desperate way
not to rely on you.

Unfortunately I've also learnt
that I no longer need you.

HARD EDGES

We speak of softness,
of water flowing,
and the kindness of the womb.
But what of the
hardened edges around the heart,
the stone crevices of the earth
where flowers refuse to grow?

MOMENTARY HAPPINESS

Happiness is a luxury
we can hold momentarily,
like a pale-disk sun
on a frosty winter day.
It crumbles and it cracks
and dissolves through
outstretched fingers,
happiness gone,
emptiness remains.

WEAKNESS

And it is at my weakest state
that all my demons come out to play
and prey at all I know
and have come to understand.
How foolish it is to think
we are impervious to attack.

REMLNDERS

Unbidden they come
these derelict fragments of old
unearthed from old hiding places
meant to be forgotten.
They linger long past expiry
when frost has set in but
dead leaves haven't blown away.
Here they remain, reminders
unbidden and unsought for.

OF HUMAN HEARTS

Human hearts are just that:
made of muscle, run by blood,
fully human and prone to break
It is not to be used one time
and discarded like trash.
It is not something to overcome
like another hurdle on the path.

ADULTHOOD (Part LL)

And perhaps I have outgrown
that which once haunted my steps,
lingered over my soul
a predatory ghost with no place to go.
My hurts are but a faded memory,
a stain that reveals and conceals
but no longer inflicts as it once did.

—Oh, how I've grown (up)

About the Author

Lianne M. Bernardo is from Canada. She has previously written for high school and university publications, online e-zines, and Youth Speak News at the Catholic Register whilst accumulating a stack of unpublished content ranging from novel-length stories to poetry.

You can follow her on Instagram at *@shallibeapoetinstead*

Also By The Author

Shall I Be a Poet Instead?

Of Frost and Fury: Poems Written in the Land of Volcanoes and Giants

With Quiet Ardency

www.ingramcontent.com/pod-product-compliance
Lightning Source LLC
Chambersburg PA
CBHW030111070426

42448CB00036B/644